OVARIAN CANCER

My Walk With It

by

ANTOINETTE GALLELLI

ISBN: 1483931994
ISBN 13: 9781483931999

To the women out there with ovarian cancer. This book is written in an effort to get the word out about what we are going through with this illness. Many of the things I have experienced and am yet to experience with ovarian cancer you may be going through as well.

Six years ago when I was diagnosed with ovarian cancer, my children went to the Internet for information on ovarian cancer. They told me there really wasn't much out there showing the ups and downs or the day-to-day life of this cancer.

I thought perhaps a snapshot of the six years that I have lived with ovarian cancer would help one understand what the everyday life of this illness is like.

A Special Thank You

To whom I refer to as my doctor throughout this book

John Christopher Elkas, MD, JD

For his exceptional care and dedication
throughout these six years.

Dedication

To my three children Eleanor, Mark and April
the greatest gifts of my life. I never could have
gone through this without their
constant love and support.

Contents

Chapter 1

A Sad Diagnosis

It was Christmas 2006, and I was attending our annual Christmas party at the Ritz Carlton Hotel in McLean, Virginia. A colleague and I planned the entire event for the company that employed us. A sit-down dinner, cash bar, and a DJ. I had the DJ play Christmas music when the doors opened for all the employees and their spouses as they entered the Ball Room. During our dinner, I requested he play the music at a lower volume so we could hear ourselves talk while we ate. During the night he played excellent dance music with Christmas songs mixed in. The last song of the night was one of my favorite songs, Louie Armstrong's "It's A Wonderful World." This was the third Christmas party I helped put together and I always ended the evening with this song.

I was busy talking to the wife of one of the employees about our families. I told her my mother had passed away earlier that year at the age of ninety-three and a half. She had a toothache, of all things, and we had it pulled. Somewhat suddenly after that she became so weak, and three months later, she died. My father died at the age of ninety from emphysema. He smoked his cigarettes well into his eighties. We were laughing about genes in the family. I told her I felt pretty sure I was going to live a long life because we had good genes in our family. I'll never forget when she looked in my eyes and said, "If cancer doesn't kill you first."

I was diagnosed with ovarian cancer six months later in June of 2007, at the age of sixty-two. I was very diligent about my yearly doctor appointments, gynecological exams, mammograms, and complete physicals. Each year I was told what excellent health I was in, that I had low blood pressure and good cholesterol, and that I did not need to take any medication. In the two years prior to my diagnosis, I told three different gynecologists and two different intern practices that I was not feeling well. Each evening I would have a backache. I love to eat, yet when I was eating dinner, I would fill up fast, feel bloated, and then be hungry an hour or two later. The gynecologist I saw for years was retiring; however, I told him how I felt and he said there was nothing wrong. Upon his retirement, I went back to see the doctor who resumed his practice. She told me my pap smear was fine and that what I was experiencing was probably age related. I then went to a different practice located in my town and that gynecologist found nothing. When my internist moved to a different location that was not convenient for me, I decided to change internists to one closer to my home. I went for a complete physical again and explained my pains and bloating. She could not find any sound reason for this.

Two years later when my daughter gave birth to my granddaughter, I agreed to take two weeks off from work to stay with her and help her at her home. The baby was born in the month of June and in Virginia it had already become very warm. While at her home, each evening I would complain that I was freezing from the air conditioning. My daughter explained that it was not cold. I didn't realize at the time that I was running a low-grade temperature.

I returned home from her house on a Sunday and was due back to work the next day. That evening I thought I was having an appendicitis attack. I had such a bad pain on the lower right side of my stomach. I took some extra strength Tylenol and went to bed. When I arrived at work the next day, I called my internist for an appointment. At 4:45 p.m. that day I went to her office. She explained to me that it sounded like a kidney infection. They took blood and a urine sample. She gave me an antibiotic and told me that they would be calling me with the results.

On Wednesday of the same week, I received a call from the internist office telling me that everything was negative and that I was just fine. I explained to the nurse that I needed to see the doctor again as soon as possible. My stomach had grown and I couldn't button the pants I usually wear, which usually are large in the waist. The appointment was set for the next day at 2:45 p.m. At that appointment, I told the doctor that something was in my stomach. I had gained no weight—in fact I lost two pounds while at my daughter's house—and yet I could not button my pants. She told me that she could order me an x-ray. I asked her if I could be scheduled for a CAT scan and she agreed. As soon as I left her office, I went to the radiology office in my town. Fortunately I was able to get an appointment for the next morning. The next morning was Friday, and I took the CAT scan and went on to work. By lunch time, I had received a call from the internist informing me that the CAT scan showed a darkening in my stomach and that I was to report immediately to the hospital emergency room. I became very alarmed and she explained to me that it probably was an infection. She told me it could travel throughout my body so I needed to be placed on an antibiotic and treated as soon as possible.

I reported to the emergency room and took along the x-ray that the radiology office had given me. That evening a doctor came in and told me I had cancer. She went on to explain that it was either colon or ovarian cancer. To determine the exact nature of the cancer she requested an oncologist be called in to review the x-ray and determine the type of cancer it was. Of course, just hearing the word cancer I immediately felt I was going to die. I was in a state of shock. I started crying, not for myself but for my children. Although they were already grown, I had been a single parent for most of their lives, and now at the age of sixty-two, I would be leaving them.

A colon specialist came in to see me, and he said that he had looked at the x-ray and I definitely did not have colon cancer. It was ovarian cancer. He offered his deepest sympathy and went on his way. I was told that I was being admitted into the hospital and that a gynecological oncologist would be in to see me in the morning. I contacted my children with the news and they also were in shock. I could hear my daughters crying over the telephone and all three children wanted to immediately come to the hospital. I explained to them I knew nothing more than what I had just told them. For them to please remain at home until tomorrow when they could visit me at the hospital. I was the kind of mother who never sat down. I was always very busy. I had worked for the government for thirty-two years, and now, retired,

I continued to work full-time for a company made up of government retirees and young people, which I just loved. How could all of this be over and my life turned upside down so fast?

A man came from transportation and wheeled me to the area of the hospital where my room was located. When we arrived, the nurse said that I would be in room 743. After helping me into the bed, she introduced herself and told me she would be my nurse for the evening. She wrote her name and telephone number on the chalkboard on the wall. It had a place on the board for remarks, and she wrote, "for the patient to feel comfortable." Another person entered the room to take my vitals, which meant taking my blood pressure and temperature. The nurse provided me with a hospital gown, towels, and a mauve-colored plastic basin. The basin contained a toothbrush, toothpaste, soap, and a pair of foot booties. Later the nurse returned with a pitcher of ice water. After explaining to me how to turn the TV on and how to buzz for assistance from the remote located on the side of my bed, she went on her way to get me something to eat. It was now eight o'clock at night and I had not eaten anything since lunch time.

Lying in the bed, I looked around the room and thought, *I can't believe this*. Then I thought of my children and my mom and dad. Again I worried about my children going through this terrible cancer with me. When I thought of my mom and dad, I was pleased for the first time that they had passed away, especially my mom. At the end of her life, why have her be saddened because one of her children had cancer? Five years prior to her death, my brother Joseph was diagnosed with kidney cancer. He had his kidney removed and he is now fine. At the time it was his decision not to tell our mom, and we respected his decision, so she never knew. He was absolutely right to do so.

Aside from having received some of the worst news the night before, the best thing that happened to me the next day in the hospital was meeting the gynecologic oncologist who turned out to be my doctor. I never selected this doctor and I had never met this doctor before. I knew nothing about him and nothing about ovarian cancer. I asked him where he went to school, where he interned, and the name of his practice. I asked him what he thought of the x-ray and what kind of surgery was he going to perform on me. I also asked how long I would be in the hospital, the complete recovery time, and exactly what happens after that. He was very warm and caring. He listened as if I was the only patient he had to all my questions, fears and concerns. He explained the procedure and I didn't feel like he rushed through anything. For some reason which is hard to describe I felt safe and at the same time hopeful. He was wonderful. I immediately liked him, and although I knew nothing about this illness, I trusted him. This is not normally the way I am, but I just felt he was the right person.

Chapter 2

The Surgery

Two days later, I was operated on. The surgery took four hours. My doctor performed what is called debulking. I was stage III; the cancer was in both ovaries, fallopian tubes (the uterus was removed when I was thirty-five years old because of a non-malignant tumor), the appendix, and 85 percent of the omentum (this is the fatty tissue that drapes between the stomach and colon). I had a total of fifty-four staples in my stomach that went vertically clear up to the center of my chest. I remained in the hospital for eight days.

My recovery in the hospital was a slow one. When I had to cough or sneeze, I held a pillow to my stomach for support. On the second day after my surgery, the nurses helped me get out of the bed. I was in great pain and it felt like my insides would fall out. One of the nurses went and got me what looked like a large ace bandage and wrapped it entirely across my stomach and around my body. This seemed to hold everything in place and I felt better. It took three days before I could get out of bed by myself and walk the halls. Daily I walked around the halls of the hospital holding the IV pole that administered antibiotics and slowly I began to gain my strength back.

Daily my doctor came to check on my progress. He would check my stomach and we would talk about how I was feeling. Along with this visit, there was a lot of traffic in the room from interns or residents who came by to check on my progress. One day I was told by one of them something that I thought was very strange. He told me we were all going to die, but the difference was that I already knew what I was going to die from. I never forgot that statement. I lay in the bed thinking about it for a long time. In the end, I disagreed. How did he know what I was going to die from? I could have a heart attack instead.

During my stay in the hospital, many of my colleagues at work wanted to come and see me. I felt so uncomfortable and looked so bad that I didn't want any visitors, with the exception of my children. I even told my children that they did not need to visit me every day. They were all busy working and the hospital was taking good care of me. To have an excellent hospital so close to where I live, with such an outstanding staff of nurses and doctors, was very comforting to me. Of course my boss Brad came anyway. He arrived one evening with his wife, pushing a stroller with his youngest baby in it. Brad was deeply moved by my illness, as his mother had passed away a few years earlier from ovarian cancer. I did take the opportunity to speak to him about Maggie, our paralegal in the office, filling in for me while I was on sick leave. It worked out perfectly, since Maggie had asked me prior to my getting sick if she could work with me. A fast learner, she did great and I was only a phone call away if needed.

The day I was released from the hospital all three of my children had taken off from work to take me home and make sure I was comfortable. I was so weak that my body shook. I had no appetite so I had very little to eat the first day home. The next day for lunch I decided to have a grilled cheese sandwich. Shortly after eating the sandwich, I started to experience pains similar to those that you would feel with an intestinal virus. I called the doctor's office and explained to them that I was in bad pain. I was advised to report to the emergency room at the hospital. Suddenly I began projectile vomiting uncontrollably. I called 911 for an ambulance and went to the hospital. The hospital administered a few tests and did a CAT scan. The results of the CAT scan showed that I had a kink in my intestines and that the food was stuck. I was then readmitted into the hospital. I was put on a liquid diet and three days later I was released to go home.

Chapter 3

Chemotherapy

A week later I had an appointment with my doctor. He explained that although he had removed all the cancer, he could see I would need to take approximately six rounds of chemotherapy. The chemotherapy of choice was Taxol and Carboplatin. Fortunately with the good health insurance I have, I was able to have this administered to me in his office in a room called the Chemo Room. The room had eight recliners and seven of the most wonderful, experienced, and caring oncology nurses that you will ever meet in your life. After he spoke to me, he brought me to the Chemo Room and one of the nurses gave me an hour briefing on what to expect when taking chemo.

CHEMOTHERAPY TIP SHEET

Rest—*Have rest periods each day.*

Drink—*plenty of fluids each day. This means a cup of fluid every hour. This will help your kidneys to work well.*

Eat—*high protein foods: fish, chicken, beans, pork and beef. Eat high calorie foods, such as milkshakes, ice cream, and sauces. These foods replace the energy your body is using to fight the cancer cells.*

For **nausea**—*take the anti-nausea medicine as directed. Sometimes you may have to take more anti-nausea medicine about a half-hour before you eat. Try smaller, more frequent meals, or snacks, instead of three big meals.*

You may be constipated or have diarrhea. For both, drink plenty of fluids. For **constipation**, *increase the amount of fiber in your diet, bran, whole-wheat breads and cereals, vegetables, and fruit.*

For **diarrhea**, *try the BRAT diet: bananas, rice, applesauce, and toast. Stay away from high-fiber foods and dairy products, like milk, cheese, or ice cream.*

Practice good **mouth care** *after eating and at bed-time, using a soft bristle toothbrush. Use a saltwater gargle at least 4 times a day.*

Take your **temperature** once a day in the evening. A rise in your temperature may mean an infection.

You may have **hair loss**. Getting a short haircut before you begin to lose your hair may help. Your hair will start to grow back after your last treatment.

Avoid large crowds and close contact with people who are sick.

CALL YOUR DOCTOR IF YOU HAVE:

Vomiting not controlled by your anti-nausea medicine.

Diarrhea more than four times a day not controlled by anti-diarrhea medicine.

Constipation greater than three days.

Sore throat, pain in your gums, or white patches on any part of your mouth.

Temperature over 100.4 F, chills, or tiredness that keeps getting worse.

Any unexplained bleeding or bruising from your skin, gums, or sputum (what you cough up).

The nurse wrote up a calendar of the times and dates the chemo would be administered, listing the doctor appointments. I would be seeing my doctor prior to each new round of chemo. I also had appointments where I would be having my blood checked and sent out to Quest Diagnostic. My blood would be taken prior to each chemo infusion to assure that my red and white cells were at a good level in order to take the chemo that day. The blood would be sent to Quest Diagnostic once a month to check for cancer cells through the CA 125 levels and a CBC (complete blood count). The office also sends blood drawings to LabCorp. I personally found that it was important to stay with the same laboratory for a consistent reading of my blood. This is not to say that one laboratory is better than the other, because this is not the case.

CA125

The CA125 is measured by your blood sample. CA stands for carbohydrate antigen, which is a protein that is a tumor marker or biomarker, because it is a substance found in greater concentration in tumor cells than in other cells in the body. CA125 is present in greater concentration in ovarian cancer cells than in other cells.

A folder was given to me at that meeting explaining what to expect when you are on chemotherapy and an explanation of both Taxol and Carboplatin.

Prior to taking the chemo, I was scheduled to have a MediPort inserted in my chest on August 6, 2007. The MediPort was inserted surgically under local anesthesia in the hospital.

MEDIPORT

*A **MediPort** is a device usually implanted by a vascular surgeon within a patient's chest. It is a device made up of elastic tubing connected to a reservoir. The catheters are introduced through a large vein deep in the chest and the reservoir is fixed to the chest wall under the skin. The MediPort allows medication and administration of chemotherapy and drawing of blood periodically without so many sticks in the arms. It is used for the majority of intravenous blood draws and the administration of medication. The device is accessed with a needle. You can shower or bathe when the needle is not in the port. You can feel and see an outline of the device as a small bump on the surface of the skin.*

Prior to my MediPort being inserted, any blood that needed to be taken was taken from my arm. It seemed we always had a problem finding a good vein. This led to a needle poking my arm several times. I highly recommend a MediPort. It beats having needles inserted in your arm to find a vein. I have never had any problems with the MediPort and think it is a wonderful device.

CHEMOTHERAPY

Chemotherapy refers to the use of drugs to treat cancer. The word Chemotherapy is a combination of two words, "chemical" and "treatment." White blood cells, red blood cells, and platelets are monitored closely during chemotherapy with blood tests called CBCs (Complete Blood Counts). Chemotherapy decreases or suppresses these cells because chemotherapy attacks rapidly dividing cells. Red blood cells, white blood cells, and platelets are all rapidly dividing cells like cancer cells.

> *White Blood Cells are important fighters of infection in the body. Your risk of infection is greater when the white blood cells are low. A very low white blood cell count is called neutropenia. White cells, specifically neutrophils, will be low for a few days as a result of chemotherapy. This usually occurs eight to fourteen days after treatment and usually improves by twenty-one days after treatment.*

Red Blood Cells *are the cells that carry oxygen to other cells and organs in your body. Red blood cells can be affected by chemotherapy. Anemia is the result of low red blood cells.*

Platelets *are cells that control the normal blood clotting process. Platelets usually decrease about eight to fourteen days after chemotherapy. Not all chemotherapy drugs affect platelets. Platelets usually recover or begin to increase by fourteen to twenty-one days. Low platelets are called thrombocytopenia.*

The protocol I was given for the chemotherapy was a total of six rounds of Taxol and Carboplatin.

TAXOL (Paclitaxel)

All cells, whether they are healthy cells or cancerous cells, go through several stages of growth. During a stage in the cell cycle known as mitosis, the cell attempts to divide. At this point, the cell already contains a miniature supporting structure, a type of cellular skeleton. This skeleton supports the cell, gives the cell its shape, and also supports other structures within the cell. Just as your skeleton must be movable for you to perform various tasks, so must the cell's skeleton be movable. Taxol "paralyzes" this support structure inside the cell. The cell is then unable to perform some of the functions necessary for growth or reproduction, so it is unable to reproduce and eventually dies.

Main Side Effects: low blood counts, nausea, hair loss, numbness and tingling of hands and feet, and joint pain. Pre-meds are given prior to administering Taxol. Taxol is given intravenously, taking approximately three hours.

CARBOPLATIN (Paraplatin)

Carboplatin kills cancer cells by binding to DNA and interfering with the cell repair mechanism, which eventually leads to cell death. It is classified as an alkylating agent. Carboplatin is used alone or in combination with other medications to treat cancer of the ovaries and other cancers. Carboplatin is given intravenously. The drug enters the bloodstream directly and begins to work immediately.

Main Side Effects: low blood count, nausea, and hair thinning. It is filtered through the kidney so oral fluid intake, especially the day before treatment and the day after must be increased. Pre-meds are given prior to administering Carboplatin, minimizing the possibility of nausea or allergic reactions. The infusion lasts approximately an hour.

I was scheduled to have my first chemo Monday at eight-thirty in the morning before the infusion of Taxol and Carboplatin, you must pre-medicate. This helps to prevent or reduce the chances of a serious allergic reaction during the administration of chemo. I took Decadron (another name for it is dexamethasone) on Sunday, five tablets of 4 mg each at nine at night and five more tablets on Monday at three in the morning. It is extremely important to take this drug at the exact time scheduled. Taking it at the incorrect time may result in an allergic reaction to the chemo. That morning before leaving for my chemo, I took one Emend and was directed to take one pill for the next two mornings. Because they would be accessing my Mediport, I placed Lidocaine/Prilocaine on top of the Mediport bump on my chest. I covered the area with a piece of Glad Cling Wrap and then placed tape over this area. This numbed the area, which would then make it less painful when the nurse inserted the needle into the Mediport to access it for treatment.

DECADRON (Dexamethasone)

Decadron belongs to the group of medications known as corticosteroids. This drug is used to treat any allergic reactions or inflammation resulting from the chemo.

Main Side Effects: Insomnia, hypertension, ulcers, flushed face.

EMEND (Aprepitant)

It is used in adults to prevent nausea and vomiting caused by highly emetogenic chemotherapy. Emend blocks the vomiting signals from the brain rather than from the stomach. When used with other anti-nausea and vomiting medications it can help chemotherapy-induced nausea for up to five days from the day chemo is given.

LIDOCAINE AND PRILOCAINE

Lidocaine and Prilocaine topical cream is used on the skin to cause numbness or loss of feeling before certain medical procedures. It is used to prevent pain caused by an injection or the drawing of blood. It deadens the nerve endings in the skin. This medicine is available only with your doctor's prescription.

Before my first chemo session, I was nervous because I did not know exactly what was going to happen. I arrived in the Chemo Room and was greeted with a hug from the nurses. I selected a recliner. My Mediport was accessed and my blood drawn via the Mediport. It was then taken down the hall to be processed through a machine to check the count of my red and white cells. A copy of this is always given to the patient, and I have saved all of mine. With the blood looking well enough for chemo, my blood pressure was then taken. They then started with the pre-medications. I was asked if I had taken the Decadron and I told them that I had. The other pre-medications were Benedril (to prevent an allergic reaction), Aloxi (prevention of nausea related to chemo), and Cimetidine (a histamine that inhibits stomach acid).

Upon completion of the pre-medication, a bag of fluids was flushed through my system. I was freezing from the cold solution going through my body. I asked the nurse if I could have a blanket. The nurse covered me up with a nice warm blanket. After this they advised me that they were starting the chemo. Unfortunately, two minutes into the infusion I yelled out that I had a terrible pain down my spine. The nurse immediately shut off the machine and another nurse ran to get a doctor. Because I was taking the chemo treatments right in my doctor's suite, there was always a doctor on duty in the next room seeing patients. My doctor happened to be in the office that day and he came immediately to the Chemo Room. He gave some orders to the nurses to administer something to me, but I was not sure what it was. The pain stopped. He then pulled up a chair and explained to me if I was unable to tolerate the Taxol treatment, he would need to change it from Taxol to Taxotere (they call it a sister of Taxol). I thought about it for a minute and then said I would like to try the Taxol again. He told the nurses to drip the chemo at a slower rate and three hours or so later it was all infused. The Carboplatin took an hour to complete after administering the Taxol and that went in just fine. My chemo session started at eight-thirty in the morning and ended shortly after two o'clock in the afternoon. I had packed a small cooler with a sandwich, water bottles, and cookies so I was set for all of those hours. Of course, I have had family members ask me since then what I do during all those hours. To tell you the truth, I become so sleepy from the Benedril that I usually sleep or drift into another world, but I am fine.

After the completion of my first chemo treatment, my daughter, on behalf of my three children, presented me with a beautiful little glass bowl from the florist that had a flower floating in it. This was to represent my first chemotherapy treatment. I might add that she presented me with a new bowl and flower thereafter for all six treatments.

The next day my face was flushed from the Decadron and I was completely ill with nausea. I called the office and told them I took some Zofran and it really didn't do anything for me. They told me to come in for some hydration.

ZOFRAN (Ondansetron)

Zofran *blocks the actions of chemicals in the body that can trigger nausea and vomiting. Zofran is used to prevent nausea and vomiting that may be caused by surgery or by medicine to treat cancer (chemotherapy or radiation).*

Hydration was a great help for me. My Mediport was accessed and a large bag of fluids was administered. Somehow I just felt better. Since the hydration offered me some nausea relief, it was then scheduled the day after all of my chemo's and sometimes clear to Friday according to how I was feeling. A few times I had it on a Saturday morning at the hospital in the Infusion Center. However, hydration did not help with the terrible metal taste in my mouth, which I was experiencing from the chemo. Very often, I had mouth sores. I asked the nurse what else could be done besides always rinsing my mouth and brushing carefully with a soft tooth brush. I was given a prescription for "Magic Mouth Wash." This solution numbed the inside surfaces of my mouth, making it less painful.

I had lost all of my hair by the second round of the chemo. Somehow to me it seemed very unimportant, as I knew when I was finished with the chemo it would grow back. I had purchased two wigs; however, most of the time I didn't wear them until I returned full time to work.

On October 7, 2007, when they tested my blood for my fourth chemo session, the red blood count was so low that I was unable to take the chemo. The nurse scheduled me in the hospital as an outpatient in the Short Stay area for a blood transfusion. This was the first blood transfusion that I had ever had.

The first time I lost my hair

After registering in the hospital and receiving my identification band with all my information (name, date of birth, etc.,), I was directed to the floor and area called Short Stay. At Short Stay, the room I was given was semi-private. Prior to receiving the blood transfusion, a technician arrived to take my blood. He put another identification band on my wrist that had identification numbers on it. You could peel sections of these off the band and place them on all the paperwork associated with the blood that I was going to receive. I was told not to remove this identification band. I had to wear it at all times. If the identification band is removed, even if you have it with you, a new blood specimen must be drawn. The specimen of blood was then taken to a laboratory where it was checked and matched for the blood that I was going to be given. This took approximately two hours. During this time, they had accessed my Mediport and started to hydrate me. The nurse explained to me the benefits and risks of receiving a blood transfusion. I then signed permission forms acknowledging I understood the risks and benefits involved. A few minutes before the arrival of the blood, I was given two tablets of extra strength Tylenol and 50 ml of Benedril. Both of these were given in pill form. When the blood arrived, two nurses asked me my name and date of birth. They both checked my identification band, reading out the numbers on the band and making sure they corresponded correctly to the numbers on my pint of blood. After this was completed, the blood tube was screwed onto the Mediport and the blood started to enter my body. It seemed like every fifteen minutes my blood pressure was taken, and they stayed in the room a very long time. One nurse kept coming in and out of my room and the other one left. After the completion of one pint of blood, another pint came up from the laboratory. Both nurses again asked me my name and date of birth and checked and called out the number on my band to ensure that it corresponded with the one on the new pint of blood.

While watching the blood enter my body, I couldn't help but think of my coworker Mark. It seemed like every eight to ten weeks he would donate his blood to the blood bank. I used to tell him he was very generous and that I would never do what he was doing. Here I was in the hospital receiving blood from someone who took the time to donate his/her blood. After Mark realized that I might be needing blood in the future, he started donating his blood in my name. My son had always donated his blood prior to my illness, but now that I was in this situation it became his mission. If the blood that one donates and designates to a particular person is not used by that person, it is then distributed to anyone prior to expiration. Also, even though blood is donated in your name, once it is checked it might not exactly match and therefore you would be unable to receive that blood. The thoughtful kindness of both my coworker Mark and my son Mark is wonderful. From beginning to end, I would say I was in the hospital for approximately seven to eight hours.

Two days after receiving the blood, my red blood cells were at a higher level, my energy level had improved and the headaches I had were gone. And so I went on to my next round of chemo.

The two chemo treatments (Taxol and Carboplatin) were very strong and hard on my body. The chemo made me very sensitive to smells and made me feel nauseous. I was light-headed and dizzy. I was unable to concentrate on anything. It was difficult for me to even read or watch television, which just seemed like noise to me. And my stomach hurt most of the time. I experienced terrible leg cramps that would awaken me from my sleep. Several times I woke up from extreme pain in my calf and it felt like my leg was knotting up like a ball. I told the nurse what was happening to me on some evenings. She told me I needed to drink more fluids. I always increased my water intake, especially before and after chemo days. Because I was so nauseous, it was difficult to do this on some of the days, so I would suck on ice pops. During this time I discovered the drug Ativan. The nurse gave me a prescription for this drug in the hopes that it might help with the nausea. This drug, although not primarily used to treat nausea, seemed to help me a great deal with my nausea.

ATIVAN (Adavan)

ATIVAN (Lorazepam) is a benzodiazepine. Ativan works by slowing down the movement of chemicals in the brain. This results in a reduction in nervous tension (anxiety) and causes little sedation. Ativan (Adavan) is used to treat anxiety associated with symptoms of depression. It is also used to treat nausea and vomiting. Ativan (Adavan) may be habit forming.

It took a good five months to complete all six rounds of Taxol and Carboplatin. During this time, I was also given Neupogen (Filgrastim) shots to help my white blood cells stay up, as they were dangerously low.

NEUPOGEN (Filgrastim)

In the body's bone marrow (the soft, sponge-like material found inside bones) blood cells are produced. As described earlier in the book, there are three major types of blood cells—white blood cells, which fight infection; red blood cells, which carry oxygen to and remove waste products from organs and tissues; and platelets, which enable the blood to clot. Cancer treatments, such as chemotherapy and radiation therapy, can affect these cells, putting a person at risk for developing infections, anemia, and bleeding problems. Colony-stimulating factors are substances that stimulate the production of blood cells and promote their ability to func-tion. They do not directly affect tumors but through their role in stimulating blood cells they can be helpful as support of the person's immune system during cancer treatment.

Neupogen is a growth factor that stimulates the produc-tion, maturation, and activation of neutrophils. Neupogen also stimulates the release of neutrophils (a type of white blood cell) from the bone marrow. In patients receiving che-motherapy, neupogen can accelerate the recovery of neutro-phils, reducing the neutropenic phase (the time in which people are susceptible to infection).

When my white blood counts are low I make a point of not seeing my grandchildren. Young children are like little germ factories and in an effort to keep myself free of a cold, I don't visit with them or have anyone else in my home who may have a cold. During this time I always wear a surgical mask if outdoors.

Chapter 4

Remission

The National Cancer Institute, part of the National Institutes of Health (NIH), maintains a thorough dictionary of cancer terms, and each of the Health Talk cancer networks also contains a glossary.

One area of particular interest is the question of the difference between cancer cure and cancer remission. Doctors almost never use the term *cure*; rather, they usually talk about *remission*.

Complete remission means that there are no symptoms and no signs that can be identified to indicate the presence of cancer. However, even when a person is in remission, there may be microscopic collections of cancer cells that cannot be identified by current techniques. This means that even if a person is in remission, they may at some future time experience a recurrence of their cancer.

At last the months went by and I was in remission. My CA125 was at a four and holding. Upon completion of all my six chemo rounds, I was given a CAT scan, which showed no sign of cancer. How very exciting. While in remission, I would still go to the Chemo Room at my doctor's office once a month to have my blood counts checked. The red/white cells and of course the CA125 were all forwarded to Quest Diagnostic for the results. I visited with my doctor every second month. Each time I would enter the Chemo Room to have my blood tested, I would look around the room at all those ladies taking chemo and all the wonderful nurses helping them, and I would feel somewhat guilty that I was in remission. That might sound crazy but I felt that deeply in my heart.

Some of the exciting things about remission were that my hair started to grow back, my taste buds were getting back to normal, and I returned full-time to work. I just loved working and getting back to a normal routine and to a somewhat normal life again. I did find myself at times struggling to remember different things. Taking chemo definitely gives you "Chemo Brain." The chemo caused my feet and the tip of my fingers to feel numb, a condition called neuropathy. My fingers did improve after some time but my toes never did. My hair grew back totally different than the way it was before. I had colored my hair for so many years that I didn't realize how very gray my hair was. And prior to losing my hair, it always had a wave in it. Now that it was growing back it was extremely curly, to the point that I could not control it.

I wore the two wigs I had purchased to work until my hair was at a length so that I no longer needed the wigs. We had some fun when I was wearing the wigs. My boss at work always told me the wig was on crooked and we would just have fun with it. One day I removed it from my head and placed it on his desk—I certainly could hear my name being called out when he arrived in his office.

Life was wonderful. I could go out again without feeling dizzy or sick to my stomach. My family dinners were on again with all my children and grandchildren at the house. Even when I was taking the chemo I always felt I would try hard to enjoy any day I could. Unfortunately, these were the cards I was dealt, with this terrible cancer, and I was not going to let it destroy my spirit, but I must say being in remission was over-the-hill exciting.

While in remission I also scheduled a mammogram, a bone density test, and a colonoscopy. The screening for the colonoscopy and the mammogram revealed that everything looked just fine. The bone density test showed that my bones (surprisingly) had not gotten any worse since my last testing.

Chapter 5

BRCA2

During this time, my doctor suggested that since I was not on chemo I may want to meet with a Genetic Counselor. I thought it was a wonderful idea. I met with the manager of the Genetic Counseling Program, and she gave me paperwork to fill out with questions concerning my health and the health of my siblings, my mother and father, and my cousins. After the paperwork was completed, I gave it back to her. I reported to the blood bank where they took my blood for testing. The test results stated that analysis of my blood sample revealed that I had a mutation in the BRCA2 gene called "4512insT." No mutations were detected in the BRCA1 gene. The genetic test helped explain to me why I developed ovarian cancer at the age of sixty-two. It also alerted me to other facts, such as that I have a risk of developing another cancer such as breast cancer. It went on to state that my daughters, son, brothers, and sisters each have a 50 percent (one in two) chance to have inherited the BRCA2 mutation. My nieces and nephews were also at risk to have inherited the mutation. I inherited the BRCA2 mutation from either my mother or my father. Figuring out which parent you inherited the mutation from will determine whether your maternal or paternal cousins are at risk to also be mutation carriers. Your cousins can pursue genetic testing to definitively determine whether they have inherited the BRCA2 mutation. If one of your cousins tests positive for the gene mutation that information would clarify from which side of the family you inherited the mutation. For instance, if one of your paternal cousin's tests positive for the mutation then you inherited the mutation from your father and your material relatives would not be at risk for the gene mutation.

I was pleased to get this information and advised my children that they too should be tested. It is a simple procedure determined by either a blood test or just having your mouth swabbed. Both of my daughters tested positive for the BRCA2 gene. The advantage is that now they know what to do to avoid getting this terrible cancer.

The BRCA2

*The **BRCA2** gene helps to suppress the growth of cancerous tumors, particularly in the breast and ovaries. Mutations in the BRCA2 gene impair its function, thus increasing the* risk of developing cancer. Having a BRCA2 gene mutation is **not** a guarantee that cancer will develop; however, compared to the general population, there is a significantly increased chance of developing certain cancers.

Men and women with a BRCA2 mutation have up to a 5 percent risk of developing other rare cancers. Cancers of the pancreas, stomach, gallbladder, bile duct, hematopoietic (blood cell) system, as well as melanoma have been observed in families with a BRCA2 mutation.

Chapter 6

Ovarian Cancer Returns

On February 28, 2009, I went to work as usual feeling perfectly fine, but by ten o'clock that morning something began to happen. I was experiencing terrible pains in my stomach. I called my doctor's office and told them what was happening to me, and they advised me to report to the hospital. They told me my doctor was at the hospital performing surgery and that they would advise him of my condition and tell him I would be in the emergency room. When I arrived at the hospital, the emergency room was so crowded that they had no rooms available. They placed me on a gurney in the hallway of the emergency room. Unfortunately, my pains increased and then I began to vomit over and over again. Suddenly a very nice doctor appeared looking for a red coat. When he inquired as to what room I was assigned, the nurse in charge advised him I was in the hallway and she remembered I had a red coat. My red coat was folded alongside me. He looked at the coat and asked my name. He then told me that my doctor was in surgery; however, he knew I was down here and would be ordering a CAT scan. I was very moved that my doctor had sent this doctor down to the crowded area looking for me to give me this bit of news. I always felt so cared for and safe with my doctor.

The CAT scan showed a hernia and some kinks in my intestines. At midnight, I was scheduled for surgery. While in pre-op with the basin close by my side, I was still vomiting. The nurse came in and asked where my family members were. I told her that my one daughter (who is first in line for my care) was in Florida on business with her company. My son was fighting an intestinal flu and my other daughter's child was sick. I didn't even inform them I was in the hospital or going in for surgery. I knew they would come to the hospital even though they were sick and I didn't want this to happen. She told me I had to contact a family member to come to the hospital before I could be moved into the operating room. I called my brother Joseph who lives in Bethesda. He and his wife Nancy were wonderful, and they came immediately at that time of night. They stayed while I was being operated on and spoke to my doctor after the surgery.

Prior to the operation, we really thought it was only a hernia that had somehow gone bad. It was truly shocking when the operation revealed that the cancer was actively back. My time in remission was over. I had lasted only eighteen months in remission. My doctor saw what looked like sawdust all over—all of which was cancer. The CAT scan was not able to pick this up, so it was an unhappy shock. My doctor called my daughter in Florida and informed her of the results of the surgery.

During surgery, my doctor removed the previous scar on my stomach, cutting over it. Upon completion of the surgery, I again had approximately fifty-four staples. There were also two drainage tubes coming out of my stomach, which were removed before I left the hospital. For some reason that I don't really know, I didn't seem to suffer as much as I did the first time I had major surgery. I was in the hospital for a week.

After recovering from the surgery, I was put back on the chemo with Taxol and Carboplatin. I was disappointed that the cancer was back and I was facing these very strong treatments again. I knew in my heart that the chemo would be the only thing that would keep me alive.

My theory was to enjoy every day like I did when I was in remission. It was much harder, of course, but there were many holidays, birthdays, and just great days that made this possible. I was realistic, though, knowing that this cancer was eventually going to get me. But I knew one thing—I was going to give it my best fight.

At the age of twenty-one, I had transferred jobs from the Brooklyn Navy yard to the National Institutes of Health (NIH), in Bethesda, Maryland. I worked in one of the outer buildings called Allergy and Infectious Diseases. On the grounds is a large building called the Clinical Center where patients from all over the United States—and some from overseas—came in the hopes of NIH finding a cure for their illnesses. It was at this time that I decided I wanted to work as a Red Cross Volunteer one night a week at the Clinical Center, specifically with children. Of course, the first night on duty they sent me across the street to the Navy Medical Center. They asked if I would visit with the wounded soldiers coming back from the Vietnam war and write letters home for them. After that evening, I told the head of the volunteer department that I would no longer be volunteering if I could not work with the children at the Clinical Center. And so I was sent to the Clinical Center. Every Tuesday evening at five when I got off work, I would eat a sandwich, go to the ladies room, change into my uniform, and head over to the Clinical Center. I learned a lot about illness there and the strength of children. For one thing, the children always had smiles on their faces and they all seemed so brave. I was told by the Red Cross never to pick up a child because I had no insurance covering me in case I dropped one. I was also told never ask a child what illness they had.

Each Tuesday night, I would go to the Clinical Center, walk through the hallways, speak to the nurses, and pick up a total of three children. I always took one in a wheel chair and two that could walk. I never asked what their illnesses were. I didn't have to—they would tell you themselves without you asking. They would converse among themselves about what they had. I would take them up to the fourteenth floor via the elevator where each Tuesday night was play night. There was something for every occasion going on, activities of all kinds. It was wonderful. One night as I went through the hallways picking up my three kids, the little boy (he was no more than five years old) I had just picked up looked at me and pointed down one of the hallways. He said, "Do you see that hallway?" I said yes, and he said, "my friend went down there and never came back." He then told me he never wanted to go down that hallway. I didn't know what to say.

I worked for two and a half years at the Clinical Center until I became pregnant and started dreaming of sick babies. At that point, I stopped my volunteering.

Now I am sick with this cancer. I am sure many of those children had cancer. I have received and still receive so many Get Well cards, Novena, and Mass cards in my name to get well from friends and family alike. In particular, one of my dearest friends in Brooklyn, New York, a nun named, Sister Mary Anna O'Brien from Regina Pacis Catholic Church presents my name to the altar each morning at mass. She calls me weekly, keeping up with how I am feeling. She is indeed not just a friend, but truly a gift from God. She tells me she is praying for a miracle. I appreciate her praying for me and for everyone with cancer. But I did tell her I do not want a miracle. I know this sounds terrible, but those beautiful little children that I saw during my two and a half years at the Clinical Center did something to me. I am sure the Clinical Center is still filled with these children, and a miracle really needs to go to a child. I mean it from the heart. If you ever want your heart broken, just look at a child with a terminal illness.

Regina Pacis Catholic Church

Thinking in the terms of the entire illness, I decided to call the funeral home in my town and ask them if I could have an appointment with them at my house. The young lady who came was so informative and didn't make me feel like I was acting in haste. She explained to me that they have many customers who make all their funeral arrangements prior to even facing something like what I was facing. I told her I didn't want this responsibility or expense to fall on my children—it just wasn't right. I picked out everything and gave the details of what I desired. After adding up the expenses, I was put on a budget plan where I had a year to pay for everything. I didn't realize that the money for the funeral goes into an account under my name that earns yearly interest. At the end of each year I receive a statement and all the interest earned is then added to my income and taxed, which I am happy to pay. I then contacted the cemetery in Brooklyn, New York where I wish to be buried and made all the arrangements with them. The money situation was exactly the same as here in Virginia. A year later after everything was all paid for I must say I felt great and still do.

Taking Taxol and Carboplatin a second time turned out to be more difficult than the first. My body was not in the same shape as the first go around. For one thing, my blood counts were not as high even though I had eighteen months without chemo. The nausea this time was much greater, so the hydration days lasted all week, and sometimes when the doctor's office was closed on a Saturday, I reported to the hospital for hydration. My loss of energy was more pronounced and I suffered terribly from constipation. My sleeping at night was all of four hours and the anxiety increased. My hearing suffered and I now needed things a little louder in order to hear them clearly. Also, when sitting in a quiet place, I could hear a constant humming in my ears. I was unable to eat oat cereal, vegetables, salads, or beef meats. I had a permanent kink in my intestines, which made it difficult to digest certain foods. Of course, I lost my hair again, but this was the least of my concern. There were times when I felt I might just die from these drugs.

Constipation is a really big problem when on chemo. Between the chemo, anti-nausea medication, and steroids, it seemed I was always constipated—something I never suffered from prior to cancer. The recommendation to combat this is an increase in fluids and fiber, vegetables, fruits, nuts, raisins, prunes, and bran. Unfortunately, I could not eat any of these products because my stomach could not digest them. So I continually took Senokot or Dulcolax and Colace. I was so backed up one time that I suffered from terrible pain and was admitted into the hospital. The hospital gave me two different types of medications, which were both in suppository form to help with this constipation but neither worked. How embarrassing it was when my doctor came to see me and told me they were going to have to do it the old-fashioned way. So the nurse came with the enema bag filled of warm soap water and of course it worked.

Later on that evening I had difficulty sleeping. It was two in the morning and I had the lights on in the room. The nurse came in and asked if something was wrong. I told her I couldn't sleep. She offered to see if she could give me something to sleep, but I told her I didn't want anything. I did want to know something. I told her to tell me what happens at the end with ovarian cancer. I explained to her I wasn't afraid of dying, but I was frightened by the thought of going through pain. I now have pains in my stomach and sometimes things just flare up that I have no control over. She was wonderful, describing to me how comfortable they would make me feel. I would be placed on a morphine drip and would experience no pain. It would be very peaceful and the care would be very dignified. The conversation really eased my mind because I had no idea how they treated you during your last days. We then went on to talk about our children and I just felt very relaxed.

By the end of March, I was back in the hospital for a short visit to receive another blood transfusion. During this time, I was so weak that going down the stairs in my home I slipped and fell. My right foot swelled and turned blue. I made an appointment to see an orthopedic doctor who x-rayed my foot and advised me that I had a broken bone in my right foot. He placed my foot in a soft walking cast that I was able to remove in the evening. The cast was a boot on my foot and it went up to just under my knee. After six weeks, I was re x-rayed and the cast was removed.

As directed from day one of starting chemo, I would always check my temperature at about four o'clock in the afternoon. Sometimes after taking chemo, I would run a little temperature; however, as long as it was no higher than 100.4, I did not need to call it into the doctor's office. Just when I thought I would feel better because I was able to walk without a soft cast on, I started to run a temperature. Each day it went a little higher; finally it was at 101 and then it was 103. I called it in and was directed to go to the emergency room and then was admitted into the hospital. A CAT scan was performed in the hospital, and via the CAT scan, they could see abdominal fluid in the anterior abdominal wall. The next day I was scheduled for a procedure to remove the fluid from my stomach. I was concerned about my recently broken foot. Perhaps when they lift me off the operating table they might drag my foot. I decided to put a sock on the foot that was recently broken and a bootie (administered by the hospital) on the other foot. When I arrived in the operating room, the doctors looked at my feet and asked, "What's with the different design?" I explained that I was concerned with them touching my recently broken foot. They laughed and told me that they wouldn't be working on that end.

Under sterile conditions, local anesthesia, and intravenous analgesia, an 18-gauge needle was advanced into the collection. A multisidenole 10 French catheter was thereafter inserted. Approximately 400–500 cc of serosanguineous material was removed. A sample was sent for gram stain and culture.

While in the hospital, my doctor, who was making his daily rounds, visited with me and noticed my right leg looked swollen. I told him that my right foot was broken and that it probably was from that. He ordered a Doppler test on my leg only to find out that I had a blood clot in the leg.

VENOUS ULTRASOUND OF THE LEGS (LOWER EXTREMITY DOPPLER)

This type of ultrasound shows if there is a blockage in a leg vein. Such blockages are usually caused by blood clots, which can be dangerous and even life threatening if they break loose and travel through the blood to the lungs.

The test consists of squirting some clear jelly onto the inside of one thigh to help the ultrasound sensor slide around easily, and then a technician places the sensor against your skin. Once in place, an image appears on a video screen, and the technician moves the sensor up and down along the leg—from the groin to the calf—to view the veins from different angles. The examiner presses the sensor onto your skin firmly every few inches to see if the vein changes shape under pressure. The other leg is then checked the same way. The machine measures the blood flowing through a vein. It makes a swishing noise in time with the rhythm of your heartbeat. This test takes fifteen to thirty minutes.

I was already on Coumadin, which is a blood thinner, to help prevent me from just this thing. While in the hospital they stopped the Coumadin and starting injecting me with Lovenox. I was thankful my doctor was observant enough to see the swelling in my leg because it really wasn't very swollen. I didn't know it was anything serious.

COUMADIN (Warfarin)

Is an anticoagulant (blood thinner). It reduces the formation of blood clots.

LOVENOX (Enoxaparin)

Is an anticoagulant that helps prevent the formation of blood clots. Lovenox is used to treat or prevent a type of blood clot called deep vein thrombosis (DVT), which can lead to blood clots in the lungs (pulmonary embolism). A DVT can occur after certain types of surgery, or in people who are bedridden due to a prolonged illness.

Finally, the temperature was gone, and I was released from the hospital. I was told to continue the Coumadin after returning home. A pigtail catheter draining the deeper collection of fluid that had caused the temperature I originally went to the hospital for remained in my stomach. The drainage catheter remained in place for two months. The tube hung down with the bag on the end. I had this tube strapped to my left leg. Each day I would empty the drainage into a cup that measured the amount of fluid removed for the day. A written record was kept with the fluid amounts and reported weekly to a nurse at the hospital. After cleaning the area, new gauze was placed on the top of the incision that held the tube in my stomach in place.

Unfortunately at this time I was so weak I could not attend the "Run/Walk to Break the Silence on Ovarian Cancer," which is sponsored every May by the National Ovarian Cancer Coalition of the Northern Virginia Chapter. We registered months ago for this event. My daughters picked up our shirts and they attended the walk without me.

From May 3, 2009 to July 9, 2009, the catheter was in my anterior abdominal wall. Finally, there was no more fluid and the catheter was removed under local anesthesia.

By now I was having such a hard time with the chemo that I required another blood transfusion. Evaluating my condition, my doctor decided to discontinue the Taxol and just complete the remaining cycles with only the Carboplatin. Just having Carboplatin as a chemo was much easier on my body; however, I still suffered from the terrible taste in my mouth, nausea, and extreme weakness. Finally, bald headed and happy, all the cycles were completed.

I was retested with a CAT scan and there was no visible cancer. However, a radiology scan of any kind would not show what looked like sawdust in me; therefore, it was very important I remain on chemo. Because of this, I was then put on a chemo called Topotecan. Along with this issue, there was another: I was not marking well with the CA125 blood test. It always remained at 4 even when I was full of active cancer. Not everyone marks well with the CA125. My CA125 was still at 4, so my doctor decided that along with the blood test for the CA125, I would also be tested for HE4 blood test each month.

HE4

(Human Epididymal Protein 4) is a biomarker for the detection of ovarian cancer.

TOPOTECAN (Hycamtin)

*Is an anti-cancer ("antineoplastic" or "cytotoxic") chemo-
therapy drug. This medication is classified as a "topoisom-
erase 1 inhibitor." It is used to treat cancer of the ovaries
when other treatments have failed.*

*Main Side Effects: Low blood counts. The white and
red blood cells and platelets may temporarily decrease.
Nausea, vomiting, diarrhea, and hair loss.*

Topotecan was given to me three Mondays in a row
with the following week off. Prior to each chemo in the
Chemo Room, I was administered the pre-medications
of Benedril and Aloxi. I had no pre-medications with
this chemo to take at home. A bag of fluids was flushed
through my system and then the chemo. Because I took
chemo on Mondays and had hydration on Tuesdays,
I was only able to work part-time. I must say it was a
very tolerable chemo. I remained on this chemo for thirteen months, at which time my CA125 (always at 4)
and HE4 remained stable. I did not lose my hair even
though it was listed as a possible side effect. By now I
was like a fixture in the chemo room having been taking
chemo so often. I just adore all the nurses and ask about
their children as too they ask and talk about my children and grandchildren. Occasionally, there would be a
sad moment when a husband or family member would
come in to say hello to the nurses after their loved one

died. They usually would come with flowers, cookies and candy to thank these wonderful nurses for all the care they administered to their family member.

Because I was feeling well enough to make the trip during this time, my daughters drove me to Brooklyn, New York. I wanted to visit the Green-Wood Cemetery and see the mausoleum I had purchased.

Years earlier when my parents were alive, my dad told me he purchased a mausoleum at this cemetery. He asked me if I would like to see it with him when I came to Brooklyn and I said no. At the time, I didn't even want to think of him or my mom dying and I certainly did not want to visit a cemetery. As the limousine drove us up and around and through the cemetery on the day of his funeral I could not believe how beautiful it was. The cemetery is a 478-acre historic cemetery founded in 1838. I felt a sense of sadness that I never visited this beautiful place when my father asked me. The deeper we drove into the cemetery, the more certain I became that this is where I wanted to be buried someday. My mother sat next to me in the limousine, and I looked at her and said, "This is where I am going to be buried." She just smiled.

Upon arriving at the cemetery and viewing what I had purchased, I was very pleased. My name and picture were already placed on the gray marble. And both my cousins Mary Ann and Rose, whom I grew up with, had purchased mausoleums on either side of mine. We joked that we still would be together after we pass on.

That evening we all met for dinner. My brother Nicholas and his wife Kathy, who live in New Jersey, surprised us. When we arrived at the restaurant they were already there waiting.

This was my last trip to Brooklyn. The trip, although not a far distance away, was not an easy one, but I was thrilled to have gone. While visiting, we purchased our Italian cookies, shopped at Pestosa's for some good Italian food supplies, and went to Faccio's for the best skinny sausages in the world.

Chapter 7

Surviving through it All

Through my illness I was always aware that being in a weaken state I easily could catch a cold. I did try to stay away from anyone sick and not have the grandchildren visit even if one of them had a potential cold. Yet by the first week of December 2010, I had a terrible chest cold. I had my treatment of Topotecan as usual that Monday morning and decided by Wednesday to visit the internist concerning my cold. He examined me with his stethoscope and told me my chest sounded congested. When they took my vital signs, I was running a low-grade temperature. He ordered a chest x-ray, which was taken in his office on another floor. The results showed that I had pneumonia in my right lung. I told the internist that I would be calling my doctor to let him know about the x-ray results. He told me that he too would be calling my doctor.

After arriving home, I received a call from the hospital advising me that I was being admitted into the hospital that afternoon. Obviously, my doctor had already heard from the internist about my condition. I packed a few things and my children delivered me to the hospital. I was greeted by so many of the nurses, who by now knew me quite well. That evening my doctor arrived to see me. Per his request, they had already started administering antibiotics via my Mediport. My doctor told me that he was calling in a pulmonary specialist to check on me. Later that evening I was sent for a CAT scan of my chest. The next day the pulmonary specialist came to see me and told me that the scan confirmed I had pneumonia. She added an additional antibiotic to the one that was started the day before. The CAT scan also showed that there were a few scattered nodules primarily in the right upper lobe measuring no greater than six millimeters. This was the first time that anything was seen on my lung. I was told not to worry about the nodules at this time that they would just keep note of them making sure they do not increase or change in size. After five days I was released to go home. My temperature was normal and a prescription of an antibiotic was given to me to take at home. The discharge papers indicated that I was to complete the antibiotic and call the pulmonary specialist's office for an appointment within six weeks. As indicated, I did go in to see the specialist in six weeks, and I have had follow up visits every six months. Those little nodules have remained the same and there have been no additional nodules, which I am very pleased about.

Christmas was approaching and I was happy to be home and not in the hospital. I just love all the holidays, but Christmas is my favorite. Growing up in a large Italian family, my memories are wonderful of the holidays, especially Christmas. My brother Nicholas would always carry the Christmas tree that my parents had purchased home. My sister Katherine and I would decorate the Christmas tree, placing one strand of tinsel at a time on the tree and making sure each one hung straight. My brother Joseph would be busy painting a portrait of the Blessed Mother on the front window, and my sister Rose who played the piano so beautifully, would play all the Christmas carols. We all joined in singing. We had so many relatives and friends coming in and out of the house to eat the delicious food that we would actually run out of dinner dishes.

The Gallelli family Katherine, Joseph, Mom, Dad, Nicholas, Antoinette and Rose

Cancer has not stopped me from enjoying my favorite holiday. Except it has kind of changed how I go about it. Before, I started Christmas shopping in October. By the month of November most, if not all, of my shopping was complete. I then could spend the month of December decorating the house inside and out, baking cookies, attending Christmas parties, and just enjoying the season. Now I found myself shopping on the computer in November. It is just not the same. Things that look great on the computer are not always what you think they will be when you receive them. I would then have to return them via the mail. Forget about baking cookies—my hands hurt and my fingers just didn't work right. From two real Christmas trees, I now have a real one and an artificial one. My children now have to help me prepare the different foods, but we all still have a wonderful time.

After thirteen months on Topotecan, my HE4 started to go up. According to my doctor, this is an indication that the chemo was no longer effective. He put me on another chemo by the name of Gemzar in the hopes that my HE4 number would go down and that once down, hopefully it will remain stable for another length of time.

GEMZAR (Gemcitabine)

GEMZAR (Gemcitabine) is a chemotherapy drug used to treat a certain kind of ovarian cancer called advanced recurrent ovarian cancer. Gemzar belongs to a group of medicines called antimetabolites. Gemzar interferes with the growth of cancer cells, which are eventually destroyed. Gemzar is given by infusion through a vein. There is no pill form of Gemzar.

Main Side Effects: Flu-like symptoms, fever (within six to twelve hours of first dose), fatigue, nausea (mild), vomiting, poor appetite, and skin rash. Low blood counts. White and red blood cells and platelets may temporarily decrease (Nadir).

NADIR

Is the point in time between chemotherapy cycles when you experience low blood counts, usually lasting between ten and fourteen days.

I began Gemzar in October 2010. Gemzar certainly was not as comfortable a chemo as Topotecan was, but it was helping my HE4 go down, which was an indication that it was working. Benedril and Aloxi were administered prior to the infusion of Gemzar in the Chemo Room. There were no premedication given at home. It was administered three Mondays in a row with the following week off. I had hydration on Tuesdays and sometimes, according to how I felt, on Wednesdays and Thursdays.

One morning in January 2011, I woke with my left leg hurting. I was in severe pain with my leg by that afternoon. I was delivered to the hospital emergency room via ambulance. A CAT scan was taken and it revealed that I had a large blood clot wrapped around the muscle of my leg.

VENOUS THROMBOEMBOLISM (VTE)

Cancer is an independent risk factor for VTE. Patients with cancer are approximately four times more likely to develop VTE compared to the general population. However, it is important to recognize that this risk varies depending on the type of cancer. Certain cancers are associated with higher risk for VTE than others. Cancers associated with the highest risk for VTE include brain cancer, pancreatic cancer, stomach cancer, ovarian cancer, and hematological (blood) cancers like lymphoma and myeloma (specifically myeloma treated with certain types of chemotherapy). Examples of cancers that are associated with relatively low risk for VTE include breast and skin cancers.

The clot was actually cutting off the circulation in my leg. I was admitted into the hospital and advised that if I didn't have surgery I would lose my leg. Because the pain was so bad, I was heavily medicated. I don't remember them taking me into surgery. I was in the hospital thirty days and I don't remember much other than hearing a baby cry all the time and seeing a child walk in my room. Of course neither of these things actually happened.

The drugs to control my pain were helpful in the beginning. However, because I am sensitive to drugs, they became overpowering and should have been lowered. My children explained to the pain management doctor that I did not recognize them. I was seeing children in the room. They felt I was being given too much medication. My oldest child Eleanor had Power of Attorney. I also had a Medical Directive, which I had completed with a lawyer when I became sick with cancer. Although this existed, her request was not followed. The doctor would ask me what my pain was from one to ten—ten being the worst. I would always say ten. I was so drugged I was not equipped to answer correctly.

One day near the end of my stay in the hospital, I realized my son was sitting in a chair next to my bed. I told him I was surprised to see him and he replied he came every afternoon to see me while I was in the hospital. He explained to me that both his sisters came daily. One came every morning and the other every evening. I don't remember my children being there or anyone caring to visit. There were many times the nurses made me fold towels and wash clothes because I kept telling them I needed to fold the diapers for the babies. I don't remember any of these things.

When I was released from the hospital, I received no guidance on how to be weaned off of the narcotics. The release form stated that I was to continue the medications and follow up in two weeks at the doctor's office. I was in such poor condition, it was obvious I could not be left alone at home. My daughter Eleanor left her home and moved in with me until I was able to live alone. Thanks to my bother Nicholas, who is a pharmacist, and my doctor, I was weaned from the narcotics. Approximately every five days, I would be taken off one narcotic. I was only on these drugs for thirty days, but it turned out to be a terrible nightmare. While being taken off of the drugs each evening, things would come out of the walls and fear would come over me. I would have the sweats and then the chills. I feared going to sleep at night. In an effort to get me to sleep at night my daughter would put on *Moonstruck*. I enjoyed seeing Cher walk through the streets of Brooklyn and somehow that seemed to relax me. When I would finally fall asleep, my daughter would turn the TV off. This nightly ritual lasted two months.

Three weeks after being discharged from the hospital (I couldn't make it in two weeks as the release form indicated), my daughter took me to visit with the pain management doctor. I voiced my opinion about what had happened to me and how very upset I was. The pain management doctor's solution was to put me on a small dose of methadone. It was explained to me that I would feel much better. I said I definitely did not want to do that. After much discussion, I was given a prescription for Cymbalta. I was to return in two weeks to that office.

I was pleased to be given something other than methadone. However, after taking the Cymbalta I was having difficulty breathing. My daughter called for an ambulance and I arrived at the emergency room. After the doctor in the emergency room checked me, I was told it was definitely an allergic reaction to the Cymbalta. I was released from the hospital that evening and advised not to continue taking the Cymbalta. The withdrawal from the drugs continued a few more weeks. Slowly the symptoms from the withdrawal of these drugs disappeared. I never went back as directed to see the pain management doctor again.

CYMBALTA (Duloxetine)

Is a selective serotonin and norepinephrine reuptake inhibitor antidepressant (SSNR). It affects chemicals in the brain that may become unbalanced and cause depression. Cymbalta is used to treat major depressive disorders and general anxiety disorder. It is also used to treat chronic muscle or joint pain.

The surgeon who operated on my leg was wonderful. He really saved my leg. I went to his office weeks later. After examining me, he told me he was so pleased that I was able to walk so well. The leg is still numb and tender because of some nerve damage. Although I worry about my leg, it really seems fine.

During this entire time, I had no chemo as it was not possible due to the condition of my body. After helping myself manage and eventually get off all the narcotics, my health was improving and I resumed my Gemzar chemotherapy treatments. By October 2011, my HE4 was rising and it looked like the Gemzar was no longer working.

Because it had been a few years since my last Carboplatin chemo and my HE4 had risen so high, the next choice of chemo was to return to a stronger chemo treatment. It was decided that I would go back on Carboplatin. In the past I did very well with the

Carboplatin. It is a tough drug but it worked well in bringing down the cancer cells.

This time with Carboplatin things worked out a little differently. Pre-medications were administered as usual. Although I felt sick from the chemo because it was so strong, it was working. My taste buds were once again tasting metal because of the Carboplatin and I was very nauseous. Other than these normal occurrences from the chemo, the first two rounds of Carboplatin were uneventful. However, the third round was a disaster.

I felt very good that day and my daughter took me to have my chemo as usual. Upon bringing me for my chemo, she would then go to work. My other daughter would pick me up after the chemo treatment. If my daughter were unable to pick me up (which wasn't very often) then my son would leave work and pick me up. If he was unable to pick me up, my daughter-in-law Sarah came. That morning my daughter told me she thought she would come up to the Chemo Room with me and stay at least until they started the chemo. Occasionally she would come and sit with me until they began infusing the chemo. I felt so comfortable that I told her absolutely not, and that she should just go on to work or she would be late. Entering the Chemo Room, I received my usual hugs from those wonderful nurses. When the pre-meds were being infused into my portal, I was busy talking to AnneLiese, a patient who turned out to be a dear friend of mine. After the pre-meds were completed and I was flushed with liquids the carboplatin was administered. Two minutes into the Carboplatin, I experienced a severe pain down my spine just like I felt the first time I took Taxol. I immediately told the nurse something was happening to me. Then I felt like I couldn't breathe and I really don't remember anything after that. When I awoke I was in the hospital. I was brought to the hospital via ambulance. Upon awakening, all three of my children were in the hospital and I was told I had an allergic reaction to the Carboplatin. When my children finally were able to see me, they told me my entire body was a bright red color as if I had a terrible sun burn and my face was swollen. They also went on to say that my eyes were glazed over and looked blue instead of their original hazel color.

Because of this allergic reaction to Carboplatin, I am off of that drug for life. There is a big sign on my file that states "Allergic Reaction to Carboplatin—no more given."

Sometimes out of a bad experience something good happens. Along with administering many tests when I arrived at the hospital, they also gave me a CAT scan. The CAT scan revealed that I had a blood clot in my lung. The next day I was in surgery having an Inferior Vena Cava Filter placed inside me.

AN INFERIOR VENA CAVA FILTER PLACEMENT

An Inferior Vena Cava Filter placement is surgery to place a filter into your inferior vena cava. The inferior vena cava, or IVC, is a large blood vessel found in your abdomen (stomach). It begins at your abdomen and continues up to your heart inside your chest. The IVC brings blood from the lower parts of your body back to your heart. During the procedure, a catheter (thin plastic tube) is inserted into the blood vessels in your neck or groin. Mine was inserted through my neck. A Doppler ultrasound or a fluoroscope (x-ray) is used to guide the catheter into your IVC. The IVC filter is inserted through the catheter and into the IVC where it attaches to the walls of the vein. The catheter is pulled out after the procedure and the filter is left in. An IVC filter is a specially shaped mesh made of very thin wires. It is placed in the center of the IVC to trap blood clots going to the heart. This helps prevent the blood clots from blocking blood vessels in the lungs and causing serious problems.

There are two kinds of filters, the permanent one, which I had put in, and the temporary one, which can be removed. Because of the blood clot in my lung, my doctor made an excellent decision to have one placed in me. I have had no problems with this filter. After surgery I was given an identification card. The card stated the name of the filter, my name, the date it was implanted, and the doctor's name that performed the surgery. Along with this information, it also included the doctor's telephone number and the hospital where the surgery took place. I also received an identification medal on a chain. All of this is necessary if I decide to take a plane.

I feel protected from the blood clots reaching a very dangerous point because of this filter being in me. And I am on the Lovenox shots, which I administer to myself in the stomach each morning to help prevent the formation of blood clots. I remember asking my doctor how long I would have to be on these shots. He said forever and I certainly agree with him. Unfortunately, I cannot take the pill version of Lovenox, since I have a great deal of trouble digesting anything with my stomach.

After experiencing that terrible allergic reaction to Carboplatin I never felt relaxed again going into take another chemo session. And yet I was scheduled to continue the chemo treatments. The next chemo that I was to be given was Taxotere (as referred to in the doctor's office).

DOCETAXEL (Taxotere)

It is an anti-cancer ("antineoplastic" or "cytotoxic") chemotherapy drug. This medication is classified as a "plant alkaloid," a "taxane," and an "antimicrotubule agent." Plant alkaloids are made from plants. The plant alkaloids are cell-cycle specific. This means they attack the cells during various phases of division. Antimicrotubule agents (such as docetaxel) inhibit the microtubule structures within the cell. Microtubules are part of the cell's apparatus for dividing and replicating itself. Inhibition of these structures ultimately results in cell death.

Main Side Effects: Low white and red blood cell count. Fluid retention with weight gain, swelling of the ankles, or abdominal area. Neuropathy in fingers and toes. Nausea, mouth sores, hair loss, fatigue, weakness, and infection. Nail changes on the fingers may occur while on this chemotherapy. In extreme but rare cases nails may fall off. After treatment is finished, nails will generally grow back. Nadir: ten to fourteen days. Premedication with a corticosteroid pill starting a day prior to docetaxel infusion is given for three days to reduce the severity of fluid retention and allergic reactions. Docetaxel (Taxotere) is given through a vein. There is no pill form of docetaxel.

While on Taxotere, I lost all of my hair for a third time—something I was very used to by now. I was not expecting to experience my teeth falling out. There are no written documents supporting the side effect of teeth falling out from this chemo. I think my body was just not in a healthy condition at this time. Thinking about it, the swelling in my mouth from blisters at times might have loosened these teeth. All of the teeth I lost had root canals performed on them years ago.

In August, my first tooth fell out. It was a back molar. Years earlier, my dentist performed a root canal on this tooth. As part of the procedure, a cap from an imprint of my original tooth was then glued in place. The cap and part of the tooth remaining from the root canal broke off. The dentist advised me to fix the tooth that fell out I would need another root canal. This would take between two and three dental appointments. This many dental appointments for me in my present condition would be very difficult. Besides, I would have to stop my Lovenox shots prior to each dental visit. Lovenox could not be taken a day before or the day of the procedure. I decided since it was a back molar I would not have it replaced. The dentist pulled the remainder of the tooth (I stopped the Lovenox). Then several months later, another back molar that had previously had a root canal and cap fell out. The dentist pulled the remaining pieces of that tooth at my request and I left it empty.

During this time, my sister Katherine died of cancer. A month after I was diagnosed with ovarian cancer, she had been diagnosed with colon cancer. Though her colon cancer did return at the end of her life, she actually passed away from melanoma. The melanoma

Surviving through it All

started on the top of her head and went down her face. She passed away in three months. It really took a lot out of me. Katherine would call me every Thursday to see how I was feeling. She was always so concerned about my health many times she cried on the telephone saying you're the youngest this is not right that you are so sick. I use to tell her and she knew age had nothing to do with cancer. The fact that she died so suddenly from melanoma left me in a state of shock. I think of her every day.

After three rounds of Taxotere, my HE4 was still rising in number. It was obvious that this chemo was just not working. My doctor had no choice other than to take me off of Taxotere and put me on another chemo.

My HE4 went from 180 in July to 382 by the beginning of September 2012. I was in a state of shock. I had never had such a large increase in numbers. My doctor was very concerned with the increase and advised me that he was changing my chemo to Doxil.

DOXIL (Doxorubicin Liposomal)

It is an anti-cancer ("antineoplastic" or "cytotoxic") chemotherapy drug. It is the drug doxorubicin encapsulated in a closed lipid sphere (lipsome). Doxil is classified as an "anthracycline antibiotic."

Doxil is given by injection through a vein. Doxil is an irritant. An irritant is a chemical that can cause inflammation of the vein through which it is given. If Doxil escapes from the vein it can cause tissue damage. The nurse who gives Doxil must be carefully trained. If you experience pain or notice redness or swelling at the IV site while you are receiving Doxil, alert your health care professionals immediately. There is no pill form of Doxil.

Main Side Effects: Low white and red blood count. Nadir Hand-foot syndrome (Palmar-plantar erythrodysesthesia or PPE), skin rash, swelling, redness, pain and/or peeling of the skin on the palms of hands and soles of feet. Usually mild, starting five to six weeks after start of treatment. It may require reductions in the dose of Doxil. Mouth sores, nausea, vomiting, weakness, hair loss, constipation, poor appetite. Darkening of skin color, discoloration of nail beds. A serious but uncommon side effect of Doxil can be interference with the pumping action of the heart. You can receive only up to a certain amount of Doxil during your lifetime.

The month of September—does anyone know that September is Ovarian Cancer Month? Probably not—I didn't even know until I entered the Chemo Room and saw a large banner reading, "September is Ovarian Cancer Month." The saddest thing was that I didn't hear it on the television; in fact, I personally didn't hear it anywhere. I would hope that in time this will change. Advertising takes money and we just don't have the money that some other cancers do. Hopefully this will change in the near future.

In September 2012, I had my first chemo of Doxil. I wasn't too thrilled about going on Doxil even though I knew it was an excellent chemo. On Doxil it is very important to avoid heat on your skin. Since I am the type that is always cold and sometimes freezing, I knew this was going to be uncomfortable. I could no longer drink my hot tea in the morning. I was never a coffee drinker; I just wanted a good cup of hot tea. From a very relaxed warm shower, I went to a very fast cool shower. I needed to avoid direct sunlight, including sunny windows. The entire family room, where I spend most of my day, was all windows. So I pulled down the blinds to avoid any sunlight that might shine through the windows. Opening the oven door was tricky; I had to step back to get the heat out of the oven before I was able to remove something from the oven. The one thing that was the most heartbreaking to me was my food. I was already limited because there were so many things that my body could not digest. With this, it was no acidic foods, such as tomato-based sauces. Each week I would cook a pot of tomato sauce—being Italian it was just part of my life. I would have it with my favorite linguine; now this was definitely out. I purchased udder cream at the pharmacy and would cream both my hands and feet each evening. I did this in the hopes that my hands and feet would not start to develop cuts and blisters. I made all the lifestyle modifications in an effort to avoid any side effects.

The one thing that was wonderful about Doxil was that it was administered every twenty-eight days. I felt some kind of freedom not having to report weekly for chemo.

The first infusion of Doxil went well. There were no pre-medications that were required for me to take at home. Of course, prior to the infusion of Doxil, I was given Benedril and Aloxi via the Mediport. I was scheduled for hydration the next day due to nausea and pains in my stomach. By the second infusion of Doxil, I noticed the insides of my hands were very pink and small blisters were starting to form, and the skin along the joint areas of my fingers had started peeling. I remedied this by using more creams and I kept putting my hands under cold water. I am not sure this really helped. I was concerned because my HE4 had not yet lowered. It was explained to me that sometimes it takes as many as three cycles of the chemo to have the cancer cells drop resulting in a decrease in the HE4 reading.

I had the third infusion of Doxil on a Monday like I usually was scheduled for. The reaction to the third infusion of Doxil was different. It seemed to be much stronger than the other two infusions. I thought perhaps the Doxil was reacting like the Taxol and Carboplatin did when I was on these chemos. With each of these infusions, the chemos lap on top of each other; therefore, there is more in your body and consequently the effects of the chemo are stronger. By Saturday of that week, the inside of my mouth began to have blisters. This was not uncommon for me, since I did suffer from this with previous chemos. I decided to start rinsing with the "Magic Mouth Wash." Unfortunately, the date on the bottle was expired and it was no longer effective. No refills were indicated on the bottle so I would have to wait for Monday morning to call the office and get a refill. Monday morning I called the office and left a message that I needed a refill of "Magic Mouth Wash." This was the standard practice—that you call into the office and leave a message and one of the nurses always returns your call that day (usually within a very short period of time).

During this time I decided to go out to the nearest grocery store because I was out of milk. Being gone a short time I knew I wouldn't miss their call and if I did they were good at leaving me a message on the telephone. They had the information as to what drug store to send the prescription to.

Arriving at the grocery store, I took a wagon and walked to the back of the store where the milk section was located. Suddenly it seemed the sores in my mouth were increasing in size and going down my throat. I started to panic and decided to leave the store immediately and go next door where a pharmacy was located. I walked to the back of the pharmacy and asked one of the young clerks if she could walk me over to where the Benedril was (I didn't have any time to look around and find it myself). She walked me over, looked around, and told me that they were out of Benedril. I couldn't believe this. Immediately I left the store, got in the car, and drove to another drug store a few blocks further down. I took with me the small bottle of water I always keep in the car and entered the next pharmacy. Of course, the pharmacy is clear in the back of the store. When I arrived at the back of the store, they were very busy. There was a long line of people waiting to pick up their prescriptions. I walked in front of everyone and asked the clerk who was waiting on someone to help me because my throat was closing. Mind you I was wearing a surgical mask (so I didn't pick up any germs) and I looked terrible. I also told him I was having trouble breathing and asked him could he please help me. He replied, "Benedril is isle #...." I started yelling that I was having an allergic reaction and that I needed someone to help me. The pharmacist immediately came down and walked me to the Benedril. She opened the package and I took one of the pills with my water. Shortly after I arrived home, the nurse called from the doctor's office. I told her what had happened to me and that I just took another Benedril (this made two pills). She told me that if I didn't feel any better I should report immediately to the emergency room. I knew I was feeling better but not completely better. I didn't think the hospital was necessary.

I was scheduled to see my doctor the following day. He was noticeably upset about the news of my allergic reaction. Along with his compassion for what I experienced, I knew what he was thinking—that this would be another chemo I would no longer be able to take. Since my throat was still feeling thick, he placed me on a prescription called Methylprednisolone 4 mg Dosepk. The prescription lasted six days. It was a steroid that was administered in six pills the first day, and then in five, four, three, two, and one, respectively, on the following days. I must say it took all those days before I really started to feel a difference.

METHYLPREDNISOLONE

It is used to treat conditions such as arthritis, blood disorders, severe allergic reactions, certain cancers, eye conditions, skin/kidney/intestinal/lung disease's, and immune system disorders. It decreases your immune system's response to various diseases to reduce symptoms such as swelling, pain, and allergic type reactions. This medication is a corticosteroid hormone.

Several days later, I called the pharmacy that had told me they did not have Benedril. I thought it was important for them to know what had happened to me. I have always enjoyed shopping at this pharmacy. They told me that they certainly did have Benedril; however, it was under the generic name "Diphenhydramine" and the young clerk who was new working at the store did not recognize the name. Had I taken the time to ask one of the pharmacist for the Benedril I would have been able to purchase what I needed but I was in a panic. I told them that they needed to tell her about the generic name so that the next customer having a similar problem could be helped. They agreed and were very concerned and sorry about the situation.

Because I felt so poorly from the allergic reaction that I had just experienced, it was decided that there would be no chemo for a month. It was November so I was scheduled to see the doctor again in December.

Throughout these six years, I have had periods of time either when the chemo was stopped for a month because I was in the hospital or I just felt extremely weak. This is where good communication comes in, if you have a doctor who you can voice that you just cannot take another chemo. My doctor is so outstanding and compassionate. We discussed the issue and decided together upon the plan that we would just take a little rest for now. Everything was taken into consideration—my CA125, HE4 and my general health.

I was late in taking my flu shot, which I take every fall with my doctor's permission. After my allergic reaction subsided, I was fortunate to be able to find a pharmacy that still had flu shots available as my internist no longer had any available. I now have my flu shot for the season.

I was certain that without having chemo for at least a month, my body would definitely feel stronger. The bones and muscles that had started to ache with such pain would have a chance now to regain strength and these pains would go away or at least diminish to almost nothing as they did in the past. I was living on extra strength Tylenol for the pain. The Doxil caused my feet to have cuts along the heels that bled, and the toe nail was falling off of the big toe on my left foot. Things just seemed to be very different this time. I was so weak.

I was scheduled to see my doctor in six weeks, and six weeks later I was back in his office telling him the same thing—that I felt weak and I still had muscle and bone pain. The bone pain did decrease but the muscle pain continued. I told him how badly I was feeling and that I thought my body could not tolerate any chemo at this time. We agreed that we would hold off on the chemo and that I would see him in another six weeks. During this time, my doctor scheduled me to meet with a cancer colleague of his who was visiting in his office. Indeed he was very knowledgeable and had lots of experience like my doctor. He reviewed all three of my files (I have that many after six years), went over all the chemo's I took over the six years, and reviewed the results of each one. He asked if I had any questions and after the visit was over, he said that he agreed and was making the recommendation too that no chemo would be given at this time.

Chapter 8

It's Not Over

It is now March 2013 and I have not had any chemo given to me for three months. Because of this my HE4 is on the rise again. It has gone from 54 to 82 which is not as high as it has been in the past, but I am certain it will continue to rise. It is being watched closely and soon I will be resuming my treatments of chemo.

In one way, receiving no chemo is exciting, and in another way, it is very concerning. After all, the chemo is the thing that I felt kept my cancer down. It is nice to have a rest from the chemo, however, how long is the rest effective before there is a problem? Will it get so out of hand that it will then be difficult to push the number of cancer cells down? These are the things that are going through my mind at times. But I have so much faith and trust in my doctor that I know if something comes up he will be fast to act on it.

At least my body had the rest needed to be able to continue tolerating the chemo. I am still suffering from muscle ache and a slight shake in my body sometimes. An MRI has been scheduled on my brain just to check things out because of the way I am feeling with the shakes in my body. I also have an appointment with the internist for a complete check of my thyroid and different blood counts. This is a good time for a check-up since I am not on the chemo presently. Along with this, I will be taking my yearly mammogram.

This is just a way of life for me, and if this is what it takes to keep me alive I am going to continue with it.

There is no ending to this book as I am still fighting and will continue to fight ovarian cancer.

What did I learn in the six years that I have been fighting ovarian cancer? First and foremost, that it is important to find a gynecological oncologist who has an outstanding medical record and with whom you feel extremely comfortable. This is a big key to your success with this illness. This is the doctor who has the expertise necessary to help you fight this cancer and can perform the complex surgery involved. Note that I stressed *gynecological oncologist*—not your gynecologist, who you might feel you have known for years and are comfortable with. She/he is not the expert with this type of cancer. I feel strongly that my life has been prolonged because of the exceptional and knowledgeable care given to me by my doctor. I have never doubted anything he has ever said to me. Check the doctor who has cared for a person with a terminal illness who has lived well beyond his/her time and you will find that this doctor has to be top in his field and exceptional in many ways. Twenty-four hours a day, seven days a week, I always feel comfortable that I can leave a message for my doctor to call me. If he is not on call, the doctors in his practice, who are all excellent and have given me good care, will call back for him. I don't do anything without him knowing. You will hear all kinds of different advice from everyone. You should always check with a place that specializes in cancer or I heard of a doctor who treats with a different method. Though all your friends and family mean well, listen to your heart and stay with a plan.

The other thing I learned is that this illness is very hard on your family, as is any illness. But cancer is so life threatening, it seems to be a greater burden on all your family members especially your immediate family. In my case, this was my children. This is the part that has bothered me throughout these six years because I cannot comfort them, though I try and I cannot control what they are feeling or are going through. The illness I have I can carry but the fact that (I know) it is so draining on them at times is very heart breaking to me.

I always appreciated life, but living with ovarian cancer made me see things differently than before. Things that were so important to me at one time are not as important now.

You must believe you can keep on going and have a strong will to live. Don't be afraid to live even when there are times with this illness that it gets difficult. Try to take and to enjoy one day at a time.

I was diagnosed with ovarian cancer in the same month that my granddaughter was born. By living these six years with ovarian cancer, I was able to see her grow. We now can have a conversation together. I pick her up from school sometimes and I know she will always remember me. When I became ill, my grandsons were nine, three, and two years old. I have managed to be at most of their birthday parties. I love when they call me on the telephone (with the assistance of their parents) and tell me something like, "the Tooth Fairy left a dollar under my pillow." They are so grown up now that we all enjoy playing the game Monopoly together. And my twin grandsons were just born in October 2012; they are so beautiful and are truly miracle babies. Who can surpass that as a grandmother? I am thrilled and happy.

Life is really worth fighting for and living.

INDEX

Made in the USA
Lexington, KY
01 July 2013